# Villa Eden

## The Country-House on the Rhine

### Book VIII

*by*

Berthold Auerbach

Double 9 BOOKS

# Villa Eden
## The Country-House on the Rhine
## Book VIII
**by Berthold Auerbach**



ISBN: 978-93-68093-81-7

**Published by**

**DOUBLE 9 BOOKS**

2/13-B, Ansari Road
Daryaganj, New Delhi – 110002
info@double9books.com
www.double9books.com
Tel. 011-40042856

# ABOUT THE AUTHOR

Berthold Auerbach was a German poet and writer. He founded the German "tendency novel," which uses fiction to influence public opinion on social, political, moral, and religious issues. Moses (Moyses) Baruch Auerbach was born in Nordstetten (now Horb am Neckar), Kingdom of Württemberg. He attended the Eberhard-Ludwigs-Gymnasium. He was supposed to be a minister, but after studying philosophy in Tübingen, Munich, and Heidelberg, and growing distanced from Jewish orthodoxy through Spinoza's work, he turned to literature. Under the pseudonym "Theobald Chauber," he wrote a biography of Frederick the Great (1834-36) while a student at Heidelberg. Berthold Auerbach was a German poet and writer. He founded the German "tendency novel," which uses fiction to influence public opinion on social, political, moral, and religious issues. Moses (Moyses) Baruch Auerbach was born in Nordstetten (now Horb am Neckar), Kingdom of Württemberg. He attended the Eberhard-Ludwigs-Gymnasium. He was supposed to be a minister, but after studying philosophy in Tübingen, Munich, and Heidelberg, and growing distanced from Jewish orthodoxy through Spinoza's work, he turned to literature. Under the pseudonym "Theobald Chauber," he wrote a biography of Frederick the Great (1834-36) while a student at Heidelberg.

# CONTENTS

## CHAPTER I
## ON GOETHE'S BIRTH-DAY

The swiftly-flowing Rhine between its bends seems transformed into a lake, until, curving around the jutting mountain, it continues its course.

This is very much the case with the story we are narrating.

The Mother wanted to go straightforward to the goal she had in view, but many obstacles interposed. First came a very pressing invitation from Clodwig, for the Mother and the whole of Sonnenkamp's family to celebrate Goethe's birth-day at Wolfsgarten.

The invitation was accepted; but Frau Ceres and Fräulein Perini remained at home.

They drove to Wolfsgarten. Eric did not say it in so many words, but his eyes expressed how much he felt protected and supported by the Mother's presence, in entering the house of his friend; she seemed a living testimony that he crossed the threshold with a pure heart and a pure eye. Yet he could not suppress all anxiety in regard to his first meeting with Bella. She came with the Aunt, as far as the wood, to meet them.

Bella embraced the Mother, and again thanked her for having subjected herself to the self-denial of letting Aunt Claudine remain with her. Extending her hand to Eric, she said, with a sort of chilled look:—

"You were his first thought to-day, my young friend."

She said nothing further, and did not mention her husband's name.

Rain began to fall before they reached Wolfsgarten, and it did not cease during the whole day, so that they were confined in doors.

Clodwig was remarkably cheerful and happy, and the day passed off with a joyousness that is possible only to persons in entire leisure, and perhaps only on the banks of the Rhine.

Roland was the happiest of all; he seemed to be the life and connecting link of the company, looking up at every one, as if he would ask:—

"Why are you not as glad as I am?"

He went from the Mother to the Aunt, from her to Bella and to Clodwig, to and fro, as if he must let every one know how pleasant and home-like a circle he had found. He was in such very good spirits, that at last he said:—

"Ah! when sister Manna comes home, she will see at once that uncle, aunt, grandfather and all are here, just as if they had grown upon trees."

The inquiry was made where Pranken was.

They said he had gone to stay with an agriculturist devoted to the church, the convent-farmer, as he was called; for there was nothing, at the present day, to which an ecclesiastical coloring and characteristic was not given. Pranken had the good fortune, by this means, to be near the convent, whose lands were farmed by the agriculturist.

They assembled in the grand saloon, from which three doors opened upon the covered piazza adorned with flowers and hanging-plants, and furnished with comfortable seats.

As they were quietly sitting and chatting together, Clodwig suddenly raised his hand as a signal for them to be silent; they understood his meaning and ceased talking. He had taken out his watch, and now said:—

"This is the very moment Goethe was born. I beg," he added with a kindly glance, "I, beg Bella and Fräulein Dournay-—-"

The ladies understood what he meant, and seating themselves at the piano, played Beethoven's Overture to Egmont, arranged as a duet.

Clodwig, leaning back in his chair, listened with closed eyes; the Professorin was sitting near him, while Eric, holding Roland by the hand, was upon the piazza.

At the conclusion of the Overture, Clodwig informed them that he had been so fortunate as to know Goethe personally, and related a variety of pleasing anecdotes.

The Mother expressed her regret at never having heard the voice of the exalted genius, nor looked him in the eye, although she was old enough, at the time he died, to know what he was, even if she could not fully comprehend him. She recounted the fact of a man's coming to her father's house, as they were sitting down to dinner, and informing them that news of Goethe's death had just been brought. An elderly lady was so affected by it, that she could not sit down with them to dinner.

In the qualified view he then expressed, she had gained an acquaintance for the first time with her husband's mind; for while he held Goethe in the highest veneration, he had asserted that the Master had made poetic art too effeminate, in placing woman too directly as the central point of living interests, and giving the impression to men, that poesy and an acquaintance with it, were the province of woman, just as so many Free-thinkers, as they were styled, regarded religion as belonging peculiarly to her.

Clodwig opposed this view of Goethe; he dwelt with special emphasis upon the difficulty experienced in our modern life, which does not admit of the worship of genius, as it is termed; for this worship could be possible only where a pure manifestation of God, a theophany, was granted. When limitations were placed to this, worship was no longer possible.

It was scarcely noticed that Bella, Claudine and Herr Sonnenkamp had left the saloon, for Bella had requested Herr Sonnenkamp that he would give her some advice about the new arrangements of her conservatory.

And thus Clodwig and the Mother were now left alone in the saloon, while Eric and Roland were sitting in silence upon the piazza, and listening to Clodwig as he added, that the future would no longer, perhaps, have any formal cultus, when there was the true consecration of the spirit in actual life.

Eric and Roland listened with bated breath, as Clodwig and the Mother acknowledged to each other the influence which the Master had exerted upon the development of their life and the training of their minds. They thoroughly discussed that work too little known, "Goethe's Conversations with Eckermann," which brings us into the living, personal presence of the Master of masters. Clodwig represented that the youth of today no longer had the same veneration for Goethe; and the Professorin informed him that her deceased husband—she quoted him repeatedly—had explained this by saying, that the youth of to-day regarded themselves, first of all, as citizens, and this life as a citizen, this active influence in the State, had not dawned upon Goethe, and it was not his sphere.

They again extolled, as in an alternate chant, the influence of Goethe in enriching and in deepening their life.

Eric and Roland listened in silence; once only, Eric said in a low tone,—

"Note, Roland, this is glory, this is renown, this is the noblest good-fortune, for a man to exert such an influence that his spirit always gives fresh inspiration; that two persons shall sit in after years, and derive mutual edification from recalling what one who is dead and gone has been the means of establishing."

Roland looked into the large, gleaming eyes of Eric, who could have embraced the youth as he said,—

"For once, I am present at your devotions."

Again the two in the saloon spoke, and now Eric heard his name mentioned, as the Mother said,—

"Eric reads Goethe's poems aloud very well."

He got up at once, and was ready to do it.

Bella, Aunt Claudine, and Herr Sonnenkamp were called in, and Eric read aloud, but to-day not so well as usual, for there were many things which might be taken as the embodiment of emotions in his own heart and in that of Bella.

They sat down to dinner in an elevated frame of mind, as after a religious service.

Clodwig could not speak often enough of the good-fortune, which had led the son of one of the guests to become the life-guide of the son of another.

He plunged deeply into the consideration that one Spirit, who presided over all, had prepared and fitted the one to impart the highest he possessed to the other.

He said very naturally, that Manna ought to leave the convent, as no one could aid her to complete her education more worthily than the Mother.

Sonnenkamp and the Mother looked at each other in amazement, for another was expressing their own silent convictions.

Sonnenkamp thanked Clodwig very meekly for the deep interest he felt in his family, and said that a suggestion of Clodwig's had to him the weight of a higher command, and he hoped that the Professorin would receive it as such. She promised to undertake the charge, as her only satisfaction was in being useful.

The rain still continued. Again they assembled in the grand saloon, and now Bella displayed her proficiency in arts that no one knew her to be mistress of. She appeared, having a red velvet curtain draped about her in the Grecian style, and imitated a famous Italian player with wonderful fidelity to the life. She went out, and appeared again as a Parisian grisette; then she afterwards appeared as a Tyrolese singer, every time wholly different, and hardly recognizable.

She excited the most merriment when she imitated in succession three different beggar-women,—a Catholic, a Protestant, and a Jew. She enacted also, with the same applause, a scene in which a Catholic, a Protestant, and a Jewish woman came separately to the dentist, to have an aching tooth extracted. And without degenerating into caricature, she took off her acquaintances, all with such perfect grace and such accuracy of delineation, that words failed to express the admiration.

Clodwig said in a low tone to the Mother: "You may well be proud that she makes this exhibition before you, for she cannot be easily induced to do it in any one's presence whom she does not value highly."

Sonnenkamp added that it was a magnificent but wasteful luxury to possess such talent, and not to exhibit it to the delight of the whole world.

Eric, meanwhile, watched with a mixed feeling these dramatic representations, which he could not help admiring. How rich a nature Bella possessed! And how hard it must be for her to circumscribe her manifold activity within the narrow bounds of a limited sphere of duty! But Bella, to-day, had thrown herself into the various parts with all her energy; she desired to have every feeling and every remembrance effaced from her own and from Eric's soul. Eric had this impression, but he made no remark. Bella spoke to him once only, telling him that the Russian Prince, who was staying with Weidmann, wrote frequently to her, and desired to be remembered to him; and that he also wrote in the warmest terms of esteem concerning Roland's earlier tutor, Master Knopf.

In the emphasis which she placed upon the word tutor, Bella seemed desirous of setting up again between her and Eric the old boundary line that had disappeared.

Towards evening the rain held up, and the sun came out with that inexpressible glory of coloring only to be seen when the mountains glow, and seem transfigured with its misty beams. They immediately set out towards home.

The whole day seemed a perfect series of fantastic forms. Roland was continually giving expression to his astonishment at the versatility of the Countess; but Sonnenkamp offered his hand to the Mother, saying,—

"If agreeable to you, we will to-morrow pay a visit to my daughter."

The Mother nodded assent. Sonnenkamp was highly pleased; he had perfect confidence in the nobleness of her motives, and, for awhile, he himself experienced a like elevation. It is such a fine thing, and people are so happy in taking up with things of that sort, and it always pays well, at any rate, in making one feel comfortably.

But very soon the consciousness of his own triumphant power came uppermost; the world subserves his plans, and it is his chief delight to make people his tools and playthings, and balance himself on their shoulders. And it exactly suited his purpose that Clodwig and the Professorin adopted his own secret plan; they must now feel grateful to him for carrying out their desires, at the very time they were of service to him, and were helping him to bring to a successful issue his main design. He saw in this a confirmation of his claim to be a being of a higher species, one who disposes as he will of others, and at the same time makes them feel under obligation to him.

On the evening of his return, Sonnenkamp ordered the gardener to place the next day Manna's favorite flower, the mignonette, in every part of her room.

# CHAPTER II
# AN ISLAND PLOUGHED UP

Humility, respect, and helpful kindness were manifest in Sonnenkamp's whole demeanor, as he extended his hand to the Professorin on her getting out of the carriage; as he conducted her to the steamboat; as he looked out for a seat protected from the draught and giving an uninterrupted prospect; as he supplied all her wants and asked if there was any thing he could do for her.

The Professorin was startled when she perceived that she had forgotten a book which she had laid upon the table, intending to take it with her, but had left it there. She evaded Sonnenkamp's question what was the name of the book, for she could well imagine, that the writings of the man she held in such high veneration would not be agreeable to Sonnenkamp. She said in a joking way that she had lived so long in the society of the learned world, that even making a trip on the Rhine, in a clear, bright sunshine, she thought she must have a book with her. She must give herself up wholly to the scenery and to her own thoughts.

Sonnenkamp seated himself near her, and said in a tone of genuine emotion, that he could not but congratulate his children, nay, almost envy them, that they were to live in the society of a woman of such a youthful spirit.

The more he talked, the tenderer he became, and his eyes glistened as if moistened with tears. He frequently said that he could not speak of his youthful years, which were arid and desolate, with no gentle hand of woman to soothe him with caresses. The strong man was deeply moved, as he spoke of his childhood in words that partly veiled and partly revealed his meaning. At last he came to the main point, composing himself by a violent effort. The Professorin felt that she must first inquire into the reason why Manna had became so alienated from him. Bending down his head, he proceeded to say:—

"They may have told her something that I disdained to contradict. Were you, honored lady, to know what it was, you would without hesitation pronounce it to be a falsehood devised by the most malignant hostility."

The Professorin desired to know what was said, but he replied that if he should repeat it, he should run mad here on board the boat. His features, that had been composed and placid, were suddenly distorted in a fearful manner.

The Professorin now dwelt upon the visit that she was going to make to the Superior, the friend of her youth, and begged Herr Sonnenkamp to avoid all direct endeavor to influence his daughter in favor of herself.

"Children," she said, "must make their own friends, and they cannot receive them ready made from others. One must be careful not to intrude one's self upon them, and to wait quietly and patiently, until they come of their own accord."

Sonnenkamp considered this so judicious, that he promised not to go with her, in the first instance, to the island, but to remain at the inn on this side of the river until the Professorin should send for him.

"You are as good as you are wise," he said praisingly, for he detected as he thought in the lady's unobtrusiveness a politic motive; and he was pleased in the notion of circumventing all cunning with a deeper cunning still.

While Sonnenkamp and the Mother were sailing down the Rhine, a strange circumstance occurred on the convent-island From one end of the year to the other, no horse was to be seen upon the island, except when the ground was ploughed. The pupils in amazement pointed out to each other a plough, which a horse was drawing up and down the extreme point of the island. A noble-looking farmer in a blue blouse, and with a gray hat drawn down over his eyes, was guiding the plough. The children stood at a distance watching the plough, as if it were some novel wonder, and looked at Manna for permission to go nearer in order to observe it. She nodded permission, and they walked along the gravelled walk by the side of the field. Then the ploughman, taking off his hat, made a salutation; Manna remained standing with a fixed look as if she were under a spell. Is that not Herr von Pranken? He continued his ploughing and said nothing. As he turned the plough, to come back, he looked towards her and smiled; it was he.

"He's a splendid-looking ploughman," said one of the girls.

"And he seems so genteel," exclaimed another.

"And he has a seal ring on his finger," cried a third. "Who knows that this is not a knight in disguise!"

Manna called to the children to return with her. She went into her cell, from which the field could be overlooked, but she kept away from the window. She felt flattered that Pranken should subject himself to the most humble condition, in order to be near her, and she felt grateful to him for being so modest and considerate as not to speak to her. She debated with herself whether she should not mention it to the Superior, but she came to the conclusion that she had no right to betray Herr von Pranken's secret; besides, so far from there being any harm in it, it was the noblest tribute of respect.

Going to the window, she saw that he kept steadily at his work, and he had never seemed to her so pure and noble, so lovable as now, engaged in this rustic labor.

On the window-sill was a rose-bush with a late rose in full bloom. Looking up she caught sight of it, and took hold of the stem, thinking she would pluck and throw it to him as a sign of recognition; but just then, a lay-sister came in and informed her that a visitor had come who asked to see Manna. The rose remained on its stem.

Manna turned round and seemed perplexed. Pranken is still there ploughing. Could he be the one who was announced? or has the Countess Bella arrived? With wavering step she descended to the reception-room. The Superior introduced to her a good-looking, portly lady, saying:—

"This is my friend, Professorin Dournay, the mother of your brother's teacher."

# CHAPTER III
# "OUT OF THE WORLD, AND OUT IN THE WORLD"

The first feeling was surprise, the second, quiet confidence, as the eyes of the Professorin and Manna met; each found the other different from the preconceived image.

Manna remembered Eric's tall figure, and his resemblance to the picture of St. Anthony, and before her stood a short, fair, gray-haired woman. Frau Dournay had pictured to herself Roland's handsome sister as like him, and now she saw a slender, delicate creature, who, at first sight, gave no impression of beauty. A mole on her left cheek, and one on the right side of her upper lip, were quite conspicuous; her complexion was rather dark, and her wonderful brown eyes glowed with deep and quiet warmth upon every one who looked into them.

Manna bowed ceremoniously to the Professorin, who rose and held out her hand with maternal kindness, saying that she was very glad to become acquainted with the daughter of her host, while paying a visit to her friend, the Superior; and she added, with special emphasis, that she had been so fortunate as to become quite intimate with Manna's mother.

"Is my mother well?" asked Manna, with a sweet tone of warmth in her low and quiet voice. The Professorin told her of her mother's health, and added that the doctor said he had never known her so constantly cheerful as now.

"Now, I have a request to make," she continued in an animated tone; "since I have had the good fortune to be your parents' guest, I have insisted that the daily course of your brother's studies should not be in the least interfered with, and now let me beg you, my dear young lady, to go on with your usual occupations. I shall have the pleasure of dining with you, and after dinner, I shall be very glad if you will spare me a quarter of an hour."

"If you have any private message for Manna," said the Superior, "I will leave you together."

"I have not any private message."

Manna gave the Professorin her hand, and left the room. She did not know what to make of it all; why had she been summoned when there was so little to be said to her? It offended her a little to be so pushed about by a stranger—for the lady was a stranger. But as she walked through the long passage, she still saw before her the sincere and gentle countenance of the stranger, smiling at her as if saying, You are a strange child!

Manna returned thoughtfully to her cell; she looked out of the window and saw Pranken just entering a boat with his horse, and he was soon on the opposite shore.

"Ah, Herr von Pranken!" cried a loud voice, and the echo repeated the sound.

What voice was that?

Pranken hurried up the bank and vanished behind the willows.

Manna longed for the time when the world would be shut out from her, and no more unrest could come over her, for now she was deeply disturbed. There was Pranken; here, the tutor's mother—what did it all mean? She took her book of devotions, but could not succeed in drawing her thoughts from the subjects which occupied them.

In the mean time, the Professorin was listening to the Superior's account of Manna's strange nature, which seemed really to hold two natures within it, one, humble and submissive, almost without a will of its own; the other, struggling, defiant, and self-willed. She had a true, earnest character, too serious, perhaps, for a girl of seventeen; she was often unable to, hold her feelings under control, but who could always do that at her age? A weight lay on her spirits which was uncontrollable; it plainly had its source in the child's keen sense of the discord between her parents and its influence upon herself. The Superior asked Frau Dournay to tell her more of the characteristic peculiarities of the parents, but she evaded the subject.

The appearance, as well as the bearing, of the two ladies offered a sharp contrast. The Professorin's figure was full, and in her face there was a constant expression of wide-awake animation; her hands were round and plump; the Superior was tall and thin, her expression severe and earnest, as if just a moment before she had given some positive order, or was on the point of giving one; her hands were long and perfectly shaped. Both women had experienced hard trials: the Professorin had won a gentle, smiling content; the Superior, a complete preparation to meet all events with firm and stoical endurance.

The first greeting between these early friends, after nearly thirty years of separation, had been a strange one, the Superior not hearing, or seeming not to hear, that Frau Dournay addressed her just as she had in the old days.

"I did not think I should ever see you again in this world," she had said directly, and when the Professorin tried to recall reminiscences of their youth, she had replied that she knew the past no longer; she had destroyed all its mementoes, and recognized only a future, the sole object that ought to occupy our thoughts.

The Superior noticed that this distant manner of speaking startled her old friend, and she said, with the same composure, that she made no distinction among the relations and acquaintances of her early life; no one was nearer to her or farther from her, and that any one who could not attain this state ought not to devote herself to a spiritual life.

The Professorin felt as if she had been turned off and shown out of the house, but she was calm enough to say:—

"Yes, you always had a strength of mind which used to frighten me, but now I admire it."

The Superior smiled; then, as if angry at having been betrayed into any self-satisfaction by this civil speech, she said,—

"Dear Clara, I beg you not to tempt me into vanity. I stand at my post, and have a strict watch to keep, until the Lord of Hosts shall call me to himself. Formerly, I must confess, I did not realize that you and I lived in different worlds; in mine, it is one's duty not to rely on one's own strength."

With all this self-denial, it seemed to the Professorin that the Superior spoke of the power and the greatness of the sphere in which she moved, with that pride, or at least with that lofty self-confidence, shown by all who belong to a great and powerful community. To the Superior, on the other hand, she seemed like an isolated, detached atom, floating it knew not whither.

They soon found, however, a point on which they could sympathize, in speaking of the difficult task of educating the young.

The Superior was rich in experience, while the Professorin depended almost entirely on the precepts and opinions of her departed husband; and now that she took the attitude of a scholar, and listened gratefully, gentler thoughts rose within the Superior, who had felt that she had been somewhat harsh towards the excellent woman; and in this mood, she imparted some things that she really meant to hold back. She told Frau Dournay that, at first, Manna's position in the convent had been a very hard one, for a strange thing had happened. Her entrance into the convent seemed to bring about a revolution. Two Americans from the best families were then there, and they were not willing to sit at the same table with the Creole, for such Manna seemed; they told their fellow-pupils that, in their native country, such half-bloods always travelled in separate cars on the railroads, and, even in church, had places set apart for them. And as most of the children were from noble German families, they united in a protest against Manna's presence, without her knowing anything of it herself. While she slept, three of the pupils had examined her nails, in the presence of a nun, and as no black spots were found on them, it was proved that both parents were of pure blood. Manna was tolerated, and soon succeeded in winning the blue ribbon by her quick mind and great industry.

The Professorin held back the words which rose to her lips, for she was resolved to keep quiet and arouse no discussion; but her lips trembled as she longed to tell the Superior that it was her duty to have shown the children, by precept and example, that there can be no distinction of blood before God, and that such exclusiveness was impious and barbarous.

Frau Dournay had to exercise still more self-control when the Superior asked her to be kind enough to fold her hands when grace was said at dinner. The color flushed into her face, as she listened, and answered,—

"My husband is gone to his eternal home, and I know that when he stands before the judgment-seat the Holy Spirit will say to him: Thou hast lived according to the purest convictions of thy soul; thou hast honestly examined thyself, and hast attempted and done only what thou couldst do in all sincerity. At our table, we had no formal prayer, but before we sat down to eat and drink, each of us spent a minute in silent self-communion, and in the thought of what it really is to renew our existence from the Fountain of life; and our meal was consecrated by pure and good thoughts."

"Well, well, I did not mean to wound you," said the Superior. "I heard with sympathy that you had lost your husband, for whose sake you sacrificed yourself so nobly and gladly."

"I was happy with my husband," replied the Professorin; "our love grew stronger every day. But love for a lover or a husband is always dwelt on; there is another kind of love, which, though very different, is wonderfully fresh and noble, and I think I know it. Forgive me for saying it, but I mean that it seems as if love only rightly begins when one has a high-minded, excellent son."

"I am glad that you are so happy; but tell me sincerely whether you have not found that of ten married women, nine, at least, are unhappy."

The Professorin was silent, and the Superior continued,—

"Your silence is assent, and now look at the great difference; among a hundred nuns you find scarcely one unhappy one."

Frau Dournay was still silent; she did not wish to debate this assertion: she was a guest, and would not try to convert or correct; but the Superior seemed to try to draw her out as she asked,—

"Do you know a more unhappy position than that of a girl who knows herself, and whom others know, to be the heiress of millions? Is she to believe in the love of frail human creatures? Is she to believe that she is wooed for her own sake? There is nothing for her, but to give herself and her wealth into the hands of the Eternal. This I say to you—I know not what commission you have, and even if you have none, you can report it. We do not try to gain Manna and her future wealth, we insist that she shall go back into the world, and return to us only on her own free decision. There is neither compulsion nor intimidation on our part, but it is our duty to protect those who prefer the imperishable to the perishable, wherever they may be. Now you know all, and we will say no more on the subject."

The Superior left her, and Frau Dournay walked out alone upon the island. It seemed to her that it would be a bold act, one of unjustifiable rashness indeed, to take this child by force, even the force of affection, from this sphere where she lived at peace and wished to end her life. She stood on the shore, and almost without knowing why, allowed herself to be taken across to the main-land, where she was not a little astonished to find Herr Sonnenkamp and Herr von Pranken, taking wine together, under the shady lindens of the inn.

Pranken was dressed so strangely that she thought she was mistaken, and she was about to turn back; but she heard her name called, and approached the two men in the garden.

Sonnenkamp was in high spirits, declaring himself very fortunate to have met his friend Pranken here; he considered it a fine thing that the Baron had changed himself into a husbandman, hinting that he himself had once been something of the kind; then he said,—

"We have no secrets from our friend, will Manna go home with us, Frau Professorin?"

The Professorin replied that not a word had been said on the subject, and that it seemed hardly to be wished; it would be well to let Manna complete her time at the convent, and certainly to refrain from all compulsion.

Pranken agreed very emphatically, but Sonnenkamp was much put out; it seemed to him dreadful that his daughter should be living here in the midst of a crowd of other girls, when a free and happy life was waiting for her.

The noon-day bell rang from the Convent, and Frau Dournay said she must go back. Sonnenkamp accompanied her to the shore, and there said in a low voice:—

"Do not trouble yourself about Pranken. We will leave my daughter free in every respect."

The Professorin returned to the island; the children were already at table when she entered the dining-room; she stood with folded hands behind her chair for a few moments before seating herself. When dinner was over, and thanks had been returned, the Superior said to Manna,—

"Now go with the friend of your family."

Frau Dournay and Manna walked towards the shady grove on the upper end of the island; and Heimchen, who was quite confiding towards the Professorin, went with them; but she was quite willing to sit down with a book, under a tree, and wait till they came back for her.

"But you must not take Manna away with you," cried the child from her low seat; they both started, for the child had given utterance, from an instinctive feeling, to the fear of one and the hope of the other.

# CHAPTER IV
# THE IRON MUST ENTER THINE OWN SOUL

For a long time neither uttered a word; at last the Professorin said,—

"You seem to be called to a higher life, from having been obliged in early youth to suffer so hard an experience, and to feel deeply the discord among men."

"I? How?" asked Manna. "What do you know?" She trembled.

"I know," answered the Professorin, "that you have suffered under that cruel burden which weighs upon your great and noble father-land."

"My father-land? I? Speak more plainly."

"It pains me that I tear open a wound which is scarred over, but this scar is a mark of honor for you, and it is not your fault, my child, that you are set in the midst of this life-struggle."

"I?"

"Yes."

"How? Tell me all; what do you know?"

"I mean that it should elevate you to have been obliged to bear humiliation and bitterness in your own person; it gives you a loftier consecration."

"Tell me plainly what you mean."

With an altered tone, like the hiss of a serpent. Manna spoke sharply and angrily; her gentle eyes sparkled restlessly.

"Heaven knows," said the Professorin, "I would not wound you; no, protecting and blessing you, would I lay my hand upon you."

She tried to place her hand on Manna's head, but the girl shrank back and cried:—

"Tell me distinctly, who knows it? What do you know? Pray speak."

"I know nothing, except that you had to suffer severely on your entrance into the convent; that two American girls took you for a half-blood, and would not associate with you."

"Yes, yes, that's it! Now I know why they examined my nails, and Anna Sotway stood by, Oh, it's well! it's well! I thank thee, holy God, that thou hast suffered me to experience this. In myself, in my own person, I was to feel the suffering that a slave feels in being examined! Why did they not open my veins? I thank thee, O God! But why dost thou suffer them to worship thee, and then to scorn thee in thy creatures? Then it was not because I tried to be reverent and obedient, no, but because I was of pure blood, that I was tolerated here! Pah!"

It was a different being who spoke these words, and cried aloud in the wood:—

"Ye trees, why does each of you grow after its kind, and blossom and grow green and flourish, warmed by the same sun, and with the birds singing in your branches? Alas! alas! where am I?"

"In the right path," answered the Professorin. Manna gazed at her as if she were a spirit, and she continued:—

"A pure spirit is speaking again through you, my child; you have spoken truth. When Lessing said, 'I would not have all trees covered with the same bark,' he had no presentiment that his spirit would manifest itself anew here in the cloister, in a child just waking to life. His pure and holy spirit is between us now, my child, and I think Lessing would say: Forgive them; they will learn that God alone is constant, while the races of men are only the ever-varying, ever-returning figures of a dream."

Manna appeared hardly to have heard her, for now she grasped her arm asking:—

"Did you not tell me, that you were specially in the confidence of my mother?"

"Yes."

"And has she told you the secret too?"

"I do not understand you."

"Speak openly with me. I know all."

"Your mother has told me no secret."

Manna seized the cross on her breast convulsively, and gazed silently before her for a long time.

With heart-felt earnestness, the Professorin expressed her deep regret at having moved her so greatly, and her desire not to force herself upon her, but to be her true friend.

Manna made no answer. At last she turned and kissed the lips of her startled companion.

"I kiss the lips which have spoken the dreadful words, and all the rest. Yes, I must experience it, I, myself. I believe that I am now first consecrated as the sacrifice."

The Mother stood helpless before this enigmatical being, and Manna at last promised to be quite calm. She seated herself on a bench which stood under a fir-tree, leaned back against the tree, and gazed up at the sky.

"Why," she said to herself, "does there now come no voice to us from the air? Ah, I would so gladly follow it forth over mountain and valley, to darkness and death."

Manna wept; the Professorin reminded her of her promise to be quite calm, but the girl declared she could not, it grieved her so to be torn from this place, which she must leave, since she could not be true in it. She would be living falsely, because people had not been true to her.

Now, for the first time, the Professorin understood that Manna had known nothing of what had passed, and she shuddered at what she had done. She mourned over having so disturbed Manna's young soul, saying that she could never forgive herself. And now Manna turned, and tried to calm and console her unhappy companion.

"Believe me, pray believe me," she cried, holding up her clasped hands, "only the truth can make us free, and that is the dreadful thing, that the park, and the house, and all the splendor are lies—No, that I did not mean—but one thing I beg, do not repent, when you have left me, that you told me what you did; it does not hurt me, it helps me. Ah, I beg—it helps me. I had to know it, and it is well."

The Professorin composed herself, and as she praised Manna's truthful impulses, the girl shook her head, saying:—

"I will not be praised, I do not deserve it; I do not deserve the whole truth, for I am hiding something myself."

The Professorin felt what a heavy weight she had brought upon the child, and she explained to her how the Superior had cured her troubles, like a physician who does not tell his patient all. Manna gazed wonderingly at her, as she said:—

"I am sorry that I too have not been quite sincere with you."

"You too?"

"Yes, I have not told you that your father came here with me; that he is waiting for my return on the other shore, and hoping that you will go home with us."

Manna rose and sat down again, hastily. "The father hides from his child and sends strangers!" she murmured to herself. "Come with me to the Superior," she suddenly exclaimed.

She seized the Professorin's hand, and drew her towards the convent. Heimchen came towards them, crying:—

"No, Manna, you must not go away and leave me here alone."

"Come with us," answered Manna, taking the child by the hand.

She went to the Superior and asked permission to go with Frau Dournay to her father, who was waiting for her on the main-land.

"Send for him to come here."

"No, I would rather go to him."

Permission was granted. It was difficult for Manna to free herself from Heimchen, who could be pacified only by Manna's solemn promise to return.

Manna sat gazing into the water while they were in the boat. With Frau Dournay, she entered the garden of the inn, where they found Sonnenkamp and Pranken sitting in the shade of the arbor.

"You are going home with us?" cried Sonnenkamp to his daughter.

She received his embrace, but did not return it. Pranken greeted Manna joyfully, and as she extended her hand to him, said smiling:—

"I have hardened my hand, but my heart is still soft, perhaps too soft."

Manna cast down her eyes. There was some merry jesting about the manner in which Pranken had settled himself here in the neighborhood. He described pleasantly how his new life struck him; there was a fresh vigor in his bearing, and a tone of warm feeling in all his words. He saw with satisfaction what impression his deportment made upon Manna, who said, at last, that she believed she might speak openly before this gentleman and lady, who were not really strangers though not members of her own family. She was not yet quite resolved, but she felt a real longing to leave the convent very soon, or still better, not to return to it again, letting her father or the Professorin go over to say good-bye for her.

"May a friend say a word about it?" asked Pranken, as Sonnenkamp loudly expressed his joy.

Manna begged him to speak, and he explained that, as a friend, he would urge Manna to act properly and worthily; whatever might have passed, it was Manna's duty not to break too abruptly the close and holy ties which had united her with the convent, and, above all, with the Superior; hardness and ingratitude towards others left a weight and bitterness in the soul. He must believe, that, as Manna had entered the convent from her own wish and a pure resolve, she would leave it in all kindness and friendly feeling. It seemed to him the right course that Manna should return for a short time, to take leave of her companions and the holy sisterhood quietly and considerately. He repeated, that though he desired nothing more earnestly than to have Manna return to the outer world as soon as possible, and as fully as possible, still he considered it the duty of a friend to save from remorse and inward disquiet one to whom he stood in any near relation. There was more than excellence, there was a real nobility, in Pranken's manner as he said all this, and various were the looks and thoughts of the three who were watching him.

Sonnenkamp was angry, and yet he said to himself: "After all, aristocratic blood knows what's the proper thing."

The Professorin believed that Pranken meant to win Manna anew by these noble sentiments; Manna herself was quite subdued.

"You are right," she exclaimed, as she extended her hand and held Pranken's firmly. "You show me what is right. I thank you, and will follow your advice."

Sonnenkamp was beside himself as he saw his dearest wish again disappointed; but still greater was his astonishment, when the Professorin expressed her acquiescence.

After Manna had begged Pranken to avoid any meeting with her until she returned home, they all walked down to the shore, and the two ladies returned to the island.

Heimchen, who had wept constantly, had already been put to bed, and was still mourning that Manna had gone. Manna went to her and found her crying, and her pillow wet with tears; she dried her eyes and talked to her till she went to sleep; and while pacifying her, and promising all sorts of good things, she became calmer herself.

# CHAPTER V
# NIGHT AND MORNING AT THE CONVENT

Until it was quite late, Manna walked up and down the broad pathway on the island, holding the Superior and the Professorin by the hand. It seemed to her, that two loving potencies, each of which had its own valid claim, were contending to get possession of her.

It would be difficult to say how they came upon the topic, but the two ladies were discussing the subject of dogmatic belief. The Professorin maintained that salvability consisted in a willingness to perceive and acknowledge a wrong impulse, an error, or a transgression. The Superior agreed with this, but showed that one was always liable to return to a false view in the highest things, if a fixed and unalterable revealed doctrine, continually published anew through some infallible medium, did not provide a remedy against error; otherwise, one never knew whether he had not fallen into it afresh, and can never be freed from the pain of choosing.

The Superior had always a positive belief to fall back upon, while the Professorin was obliged to find some new basis and reason for every question that came up, which made her appear unsettled and doubtful. And this apparent indecision was increased by the feeling she had of not being justified in contending against a faith so firm and so beneficent in its influence. An unrest, like that of a spy, who, from the highest patriotic motives, inspects an enemy's camp, characterized her whole manner, and she blamed herself for having undertaken the commission. But she was now at the post, and must defend her views. Wishing to find some impregnable position, she represented to Manna that her father wanted to organize a general plan of systematic charity, and that it would be a noble vocation for her to take part in it. The Superior waited for Manna to reply, and she now said:—

"My father's donations do not fall into the right hands; we can do nothing but restore the property to him who alone has the right to determine what use shall be made of it."

There was more in Manna's reply than appeared on the surface.

The Professorin remarked that every poor man was a messenger of mercy, and every one who needed help made a demand for sacrifices; that it was not enough to bestow gifts, but one must personally devote himself to the distressed. The alms was not the important thing, but the pains which one must take on the supplicant's account. How often a man, as he goes along the street in winter, well wrapped up in his furs, bestows an alms upon a poor, freezing beggar! For him to unbutton his coat, and to look for something to give, is of more account than the gift itself, at least to the giver.

Manna answered that women could not do such a work by themselves. The Superior joined in, saying that she had advised decidedly against Manna's taking the veil, for it was to be feared that she had no true vocation for it. Then she added in a sharp tone to the Professorin:—"We are wholly indifferent to the accusation of having tried to get possession of the child's property; we do not despise the wealth, we can do a great deal of good with it; but it is the child's soul that we value, and we do not stop to inquire whether worldlings believe it or not."

The Professorin was glad to find herself at last in the cell where she was to sleep. She had never slept at a convent, and she had again the disagreeable feeling of being a traitress and a spy. She said to herself with a smile:—

"I am rejoiced now that I forgot Parker's book; it would be a fresh treachery to have and to read his words and his thoughts here in this house."

She gave up the purpose of exerting an influence over Manna, for here were prior experiences which were beyond her control, and relations that were involved in obscurity. A deep sorrow preyed upon the child, which could only be revealed at the confessional, and which perhaps there only could find relief.

The Professorin was deeply disturbed, and had troubled dreams. She seemed to be in the midst of Wallenstein's camp, and in fetters as a spy; she was being interrogated by the sergeant of the guard, when, all of a sudden, he was changed into Professor Einsiedel, who said to her:—

"Be not afraid, I have influence on every one here, I will set you at liberty."

Then she was standing in the midst of the court-circle, and all were laughing at the *vivandière*—years ago when she was a young, frolicsome girl, she had once taken that part—and now, as she met the glance of her son; she felt ashamed of her appearance.

These dreams whirled through her brain in strange confusion. She was rejoiced, on waking, to find that it was all a dream.

The hour for rising at the convent was a very early one, but long before the matin bell of the church rang, the Professorin had dressed, and stood watching from her cell the breaking day. The impressions of her troubled dreams faded like the mists on the river, which were now struggling with the dawning light. She dwelt in imagination upon the hundreds of young souls who now lay asleep, preparing to meet a peaceful future. She thought upon the nuns who had renounced life, to whom the day brought no event of personal interest, nothing but the uniform round of duty.

She shuddered as she thought of venturing to disturb such a life.

There may be many incidental and casual irregularities here, she thought, but a holy will has authority over these spirits; and at this early morning hour, a saying of her husband's recurred to her:—

"You can oppose an established positive religion only by having more religion than is embodied in it. The idea of the pure is persecuted, hunted down, obscured, in the world; and the hand must be sure of its high consecration, which ventures to attack a sanctuary of that idea."

The morning sun had become lord over the mist, shining brightly over river and mountains. The convent bell rang, and the great house was all astir.

The Professorin went down, and knelt behind a pillar; the sisters and the children assembled together.

She remained until the morning service had ended, and then going into the dining-hall, she begged Manna and the Superior to permit her to take leave. They accompanied her to the shore.

The Professorin exhorted Manna to stay at the convent, and devote herself to reflection and pure thought. She spoke with such earnestness that the Superior, taking her by the hand, uttered in a low tone what was evidently a prayer.

The Professorin perceived that her old friend was praying in her behalf. And why should there not be just as good grounds for this form, as for an inward thought and wish for another, on whom one would invoke every blessing, unexpressed in words? With a light heart, she was set over to the main-land.

Sonnenkamp was surprised that she did not have Manna with her; but she said, in explanation, that she would not interfere any farther in this matter. She went back with Sonnenkamp to the villa. On board the boat, she sketched out in full the plan of an organized system of charity, which must be so arranged that Manna could go from one sanctuary into another.

Sonnenkamp listened in silence, but in no pleasant humor. The whole world seemed to have entered into a conspiracy against him, to make of him a sanctified hypocrite.

Yesterday, Pranken had made the same demand upon him, and he had said in reply, that it was a contemptible thing for the very nobility to be desirous of playing the hypocrite; but Pranken had insisted principally upon the religious obligation.

Sonnenkamp had shrugged his shoulders, for the man kept his mask on even when he was alone with him. He only consented after Pranken had added, that, by this means, the Court would not only be justified in conferring the title of nobility, but would feel bound to do it. Here now was Frau Dournay making a similar demand; and this was so far good, that her intentions were most likely honest.

The journey home was not very animated, for they were returning from a bootless errand. Sonnenkamp was disturbed because he was called upon to do this and that, and no object had yet been accomplished.

# CHAPTER VI
# THE FORBIDDEN FRUIT IN EDEN

A strange spirit, meanwhile, made its appearance at Villa Eden. It was kept in concealment, and yet had nothing spectral; it was bright and luminous, and yet produced a great hurly-burly.

The morning after the departure of Eric's mother, Roland had gone to the vine-covered cottage, to get a book out of the library for Eric. With the simple desire of seeing how it looked now the Mother was away, he had entered the open door of her room. An open book was lying upon the table, and on the fly-leaf there was written in English: To my friend Dournay—Theodore Parker.

Roland was startled. This is the man, then, whom the Mother had spoken of as a saint a few days ago, and whom he was to get acquainted with by and by. He took the book and secreted it.

At noon, he asked permission to go and see Claus, and it was given. Eric remained at home, for he wanted to finish a letter to Professor Einsiedel that he had begun some time ago. But Roland did not go to see Claus; he sat down under the lofty willows by the river-bank, steadily reading, with occasional glances at the stream.

What does this mean? Here is a champion, an inspired one, a God-revering champion, fighting for civilization and against slavery. He read of a man, whose name was John Brown, who was hanged on the gallows at Harper's Ferry for his attempts to abolish slavery. He read and learned how Parker had prophesied a mighty struggle; and these words fell into the youth's soul like a spark of fire: "All the great charters of humanity are written in blood."

He read on and on, until he could see no longer for the darkness. And now it occurred to him that he had meant to call upon Claus, and he hurried towards the village.

Eric met him as he was going, and was very angry at being deceived.

"Where have you been?" asked Eric.

"With this man;" handing Eric the book.

Roland had eaten forbidden fruit from the tree of knowledge, and Eric was surprised to see how deep an impression had been made upon the youth. A new and difficult task was before him, to keep the youth from saying anything in his father's presence.

"Who is Brown?" inquired Roland. "Can you tell me about him?" Eric told him. He narrated the martyr's history, and dwelt with emphasis on the fact, that even in our day life is offered as a sacrifice, and that a pure self-surrender raises to the sublime even the man wearing a captain's gay uniform of the present day. He wanted to show, incidentally, that the costume of every age and every condition in life could be the symbolic expression of the highest greatness; but Roland did not go along with him, and he had the apparently difficult task of justifying, or, at least, of explaining the position of Sonnenkamp, who had incontrovertibly taken the opposite side.

"Yes, yes," exclaimed Roland; "now I remember you said, when we were with the Russian at Wolfsgarten, 'You could not imagine that a white boy and a negro boy could be comrades.' Are you, too, a friend of slavery?"

Eric tried to explain his meaning; and, while striving to reconcile the difference, he was pleased to notice how open the youth's soul was to every impression, and how tenaciously it clung to things spoken of only in a cursory and incidental way.

Eric sat with Roland until it was very late; he was obliged to satisfy his ingenuous mind, and this was almost the hardest task that had ever been laid upon him. The youth was to be made to perceive that there was another way of considering the question, one that regarded slavery as justifiable and a righteous necessity; he was never to let his father know that he considered him in the wrong, and that he had happened to become acquainted, through the Professorin, with a spirit that ought not to have been conjured up in this house. Eric called to mind his mother, who had admonished him, with reason, that he was to adopt that course of instruction for Roland which was necessary, and not that which the youth himself preferred. Circumstances now rendered it necessary to follow only that track which the youth had entered upon for himself. It was a matter of rejoicing that he had of himself struck out the path; it was just what all education proposed: and now was he to turn aside from this track, and to shatter in pieces the abiding fundamental principle. Thou shalt, and thou shalt not?

"It seems to me like a dream," Roland went on to say; "a great negro once held me in his arms; I remember distinctly all about him; I remember his woolly hair, and how I pulled him by it; his face was smooth, without any beard at all."

"The negroes have no growth of beard," added Eric, and the youth continued, dreamily:—

"I have been carried by negroes—by negroes."

He continued to repeat the word in a lower and lower tone, and then became silent. Suddenly he passed his hand over his brow, and asked,—

"Are the people who are slaves fond of their children? Do you know any song they sing?"

Eric had very little to say in reply. Roland wanted to know how all the ancient nations regarded slavery. Eric could give him only a superficial statement; he proceeded to open his letter to Professor Einsiedel, and requested that he would tell him what books treated upon the subject of slavery among the Jews, Greeks, Romans, and especially the ancient Germans.

When Roland was at last ready to go to bed, he produced Thomas à Kempis, and placed it beside Theodore Parker.

"I would like to imagine," he said, "how they would regard one another, if they stood side by side. I fancy Thomas à Kempis to be an extremely devout, refined monk; and when I imagine Theodore Parker, I think of him as a grandson or great grandson of Benjamin Franklin."

Eric was more and more amazed, for he saw how deeply Roland had thought about them both.

Thomas à Kempis makes men recluses, leads them continually into themselves, and then above the human world; Parker also leads men into themselves, but afterwards out of themselves and into the world around them.

When Roland and Eric went, the next day, to post the letter to Professor Einsiedel, they saw the boat coming up the river, on which were the Mother and Sonnenkamp. They made a signal, and repaired to the landing. Roland was astonished that Manna had not come with them, for his father had promised to bring her. Sonnenkamp went on in advance with Eric, and asked after the household. He seemed in a very bad humor.

Roland detained the Mother, and when the others were out of hearing, he asked her:—

"Did Manna tell you too that she was an Iphigenia?"

"No. What did she mean by that?"

"I don't know."

The Mother pressed her lips together; she had some idea of what she meant; she understood her lamentation, and her thankfulness to God, for having called her to endure the extreme of woe. She inquired about the connection in which the expression had been used, but Roland interrupted her by telling her that he had read the book which she had forgotten.

The Mother was startled, but felt more at ease when Roland related to her that Eric had set him right in the matter, and that he himself would be sure to keep the secret.

Nevertheless, she was deeply troubled, on reaching the villa, at having brought hither a spirit which could not dwell under the roof. The freedom of her soul was taken away, for that which she had kept in concealment had now begun to exert an influence openly. It was no longer subject to her control, and it might suddenly appear in a frightful and perplexing form.

Frau Ceres was sick again. Fräulein Perini could not be spared a moment, and sent her thanks for the kindly greeting of the Professorin and Sonnenkamp.

Like a child who is always bright and cheerful, always living in the present moment, disturbed by no confusion, and no subtleties of thought,—so appeared the Major, and every one took delight in his steadfast and natural equability. He thought it was well that Manna had not returned now; when the castle was completed, it would be just the nicest thing: out of the convent into the castle. He should be glad when they were all together again; he couldn't stand this everlasting starting off and bursting away from each other like a bomb-shell; there wasn't a better and finer place than right here in the country, and they couldn't get anywhere more than sky, and water, and mountains, and trees.

The Major cheered up the company, who were sitting at the tea-table in a strangely absent mood. The Professorin afterwards accompanied him home. She sat talking with Fräulein Milch until it was quite late, and appointed her as first assistant in the charitable organization. She seemed exactly fitted for it, as she knew everybody and everybody's circumstances. She desired that, for the first thing, a dozen sewing machines should be distributed in the surrounding villages; she would herself teach the women and girls how to use them.

The Major and Fräulein Milch accompanied the Mother back to the villa by starlight. She was refreshed and strengthened. Her soul was peaceful, and a saying of Goethe's seemed to be sounding within her:—"Thou canst not perceive what thou art by reflection, but only by seeking to perform thy duty."

She had a work before her that would uplift her and the whole neighborhood.

# CHAPTER VII
# A NEW DOOR IN THE WALL

The Professor's widow accompanied the Doctor for several days in his professional rounds. She obtained in this way, by direct observation, an insight into the country life.

She laid before Sonnenkamp a plan matured by herself and Fräulein Milch, which he very readily assented to, especially that part relating to the furnishing of sewing machines. Besides being an American "institution," this would create a good deal of talk. He made a trip to the capital himself, and bought the machines.

He took great pleasure in hearing the widow speak of the satisfaction she derived from having the ability to do so much good, formerly through the Princess, and now through Herr Sonnenkamp.

"How does it happen," he inquired of her, "that the poor, or the comparatively poor, are united together so much more closely than the rich?"

"I have never reflected upon the matter," she replied with an embarrassed smile, "but if I should now express an opinion upon it, I should say, that the rich man clings to his property, and is obliged to think of himself; he can't do otherwise. He is not permitted to survey the lot of others; his soul, his eye, if I may use the expression, does not have, the beseeching glance of him who sits forlorn by the wayside. But the poor man is hoping, waiting; he has nothing but a bundle in his hands, or probably nothing but his empty hands; he is independent of others, and dependent on them too."

Sonnenkamp was very eloquent in praise of this considerate, indulgent view, as he termed it; and the Professorin was delighted with the polite manner and the delicacy of this man, apparently so bad and selfish.

"Perhaps," she continued, blushing deeply, "perhaps we might take an illustration from the animal world."

"In what way?"

She was silent, and only replied after Sonnenkamp had repeated the question:—

"I will give you my thought, crude as it is. I was thinking of the beasts of prey who live singly; and wolves only herd together when there is some common booty to be got, the rest of the time, each living by himself. The herbivorous animals, on the contrary, live together in herds, and afford a common protection."

She interrupted herself smiling, and then continued:—

"My wisdom is of yesterday, and it is not worth very much. The field-guard, Claus, told me that, in autumn, the birds which feed upon grain assemble in flocks, but those which live upon insects do not."

Sonnenkamp was very amiable. The Professorin added in continuation:—

"But yet the granivorous birds are no more virtuous than the insectivorous; each kind lives in accordance with its own law."

Sonnenkamp became more and more charmed with the Professorin; she spread his table with viands which could not be imported from abroad, and which the garden did not supply.

The journals, day after day, now published Herr Sonnenkamp's praiseworthy endeavors to ameliorate the condition of the people. The Cabinetsräthin came, and congratulated him upon the excellent result, adding that, according to a report from her husband, this noble deed of Herr Sonnenkamp had been noticed in the highest quarter.

Sonnenkamp was now exceedingly zealous. He was anxious that there should be no intermission in the public notices, and that something should be said about him every day. Pranken, however, who had returned from his farming escapade, showed that it would be better to hold up a little, and then to come down upon the public with a fresh sensation. He had evidently heard of the good impression which the Professorin had made at the convent, and of the earnest exhortation to Manna; and when Sonnenkamp unfolded to him his plan of having the Professorin reside there permanently, he immediately assented to it.

A path was laid out from the villa to the vine-covered house, through the beautiful meadows and along the river-bank. Sonnenkamp invited the Professorin, on a certain day, to accompany him into the garden, and all the family must go with them.

A new gateway had been made in the wall which surrounded the park. Sonnenkamp said that the Professorin should be the first one to pass through it. He gave her the key, and she opened the gate. She went through it and along the pathway, followed by the whole family, and Pranken among them.

They proceeded to the vine-covered cottage, and the Professorin was amazed to find here all her household furniture, and the library of her husband arranged in good order.

Aunt Claudine was here too; for Sonnenkamp had contrived that she should be released from Clodwig.

Sonnenkamp introduced, with a sort of pride, his valet Joseph, who had made all these arrangements, as a native son of the university.

The Professorin expressed her thanks to Joseph, and shook hands with him.

Pretty soon the Major came; and when the Professorin inquired after Fräulein Milch, he stammeringly made an apology in her behalf. It was plainly wrong in his view, that Fräulein Milch should so persistently refuse to go into society.

The Professorin had not recovered from her amazement and satisfaction when Clodwig and Bella arrived. Provision had been made for a cheerful repast in the garden, and Roland gave expression to the general feeling, when he said:—

"Now I have a grandmother and an aunt, safe in their nest."

In the evening, Eric received a large package of books and a letter from Professor Einsiedel, and also a large sheet of memoranda. He commended Eric's intention of writing a treatise upon the idea and nature of slavery, as it would prove a very fertile theme.

Eric put away the books, for he regarded it as a fortunate thing that Roland's thoughts were occupied neither upon slavery nor free labor, nor any kindred topic, but with something entirely different.

The son of the Cabinetsräthin, the cadet, was now at the newly acquired country-seat, on furlough, and he exhorted Roland to be diligent, so as to be able before long to enter the military school.

Roland was now wholly bent upon entering the highest class, at the earliest possible moment. He spoke of it daily to his father and Pranken. The father one day took him aside and said:—

"My child, it is well, and I am glad that you are so diligent in getting fitted, but you will not enter—take notice, I show my respect for you by this communication; I look upon you as a grown-up and mature man."

He stopped, and Roland asked,—

"When is it that I am to enter?"

"Come nearer, and I will whisper it to you; you are to enter when you are a noble."

"I a noble? and you too?"

"Yes, all of us; and for your sake I must become ennobled, as you will see by and by. Do you feel glad at being made a noble?"

"Do you know, father, when I first began to respect nobility?"

Sonnenkamp looked at him inquiringly, and Roland continued:—

"At the railroad station, where I saw a crazy, drunken man. Everybody showed respect for him, because he was a nobleman, a baron. It is a great thing to be a nobleman."

Roland now gave an account of the meeting on the morning after his flight, and Sonnenkamp was surprised at the astonishing effect produced upon him, and at the lasting impression everything made. He now said:—

"Give me your hand, as a pledge that you will say nothing about this to your master, Eric, until I shall tell him myself. On the word of an officer."

After some delay and deliberation, Roland gave his hand.

His father now proceeded to explain to him how disagreeable it would be to enter the military school under a citizen's name, and while there to be ennobled.

Roland inquired why he was not to say anything about it to Eric.

His father refused to tell him why, demanding unconditional obedience.

And so Roland had now a two-fold secret to keep, one from his father, and the other from Eric. The youth's soul was distressed, and it found an odd expression in the question he once put to Eric:—

"Do the negroes in their native land have nobles too?"

"There are no nobles in their own right," replied Eric; "individual men belong to the nobility only when, and only so long, as others regard them as such."

Eric had thought that Roland's zeal for the military school had excluded all his former notions and speculations; but he now saw that they were still active, and had become connected with odd associations, which he could not explain to himself satisfactorily. But he took heed to make no further inquiry.

During his furlough, the son of the Cabinetsräthin was very constant in attendance upon the lessons given to Roland, and Sonnenkamp, having her sanction, proposed that the young cadet should leave the school for a time, and be instructed in company with Roland.

Roland was highly pleased with this plan, but Eric objected; and when Sonnenkamp stated to him that he had formerly desired that Roland should have a comrade who should receive instruction with him, Eric found great difficulty in explaining to him that it was now inexpedient; that the course of instruction he had undertaken with Roland was adapted exclusively to him, and that now any comradeship, and any reference to another's condition and progress, would be only a disturbing element.

Eric, by this means, alienated not only Herr Sonnenkamp and the Cabinetsräthin, but also for a time his pupil himself, who was out of humor and refractory, after the cadet had returned to the capital.

# CHAPTER VIII
# STEEL-TRAPS IN THE POETS' GARDEN

Sonnenkamp prided himself in growing the best wines; but the traditional account of the joyous celebration of the harvest-home is a mere fable. In the morning the mists were hanging far and wide over the valleys, and in the early evening they shut out the whole landscape. The leaves had fallen from the trees, and the hoar frost glistened on the bare twigs, when at last the grapes were gathered and pressed.

The Major would not allow it to be thought of for a moment, that they should omit firing their salute; he took extreme satisfaction in his two comrades, Eric and Roland, who fired at his word of command, so that the three reports sounded as one. But this was the whole celebration of the merry harvest-home.

Fires had been already made at the villa, and Sonnenkamp's pride in each stove having its own chimney was shown to be well founded. But it was a truly festive occasion when the Professorin had a fire kindled for the first time in her sitting-room. She had invited Eric and Roland to be present, and Fräulein Milch happened to be there. And as they sat together before the open fire-place, in serene and homelike content, it would be hard to say precisely what it was that made them so cheery and peaceful.

The Mother exhorted Eric to resume his habit of reading aloud, in the cosy winter evenings, some great poems, and he promised to do so. He felt that he must make some extra effort to dispel the coldness produced by his refusal to receive as a pupil the son of the Cabinetsräthin.

Sonnenkamp, who had an extensive hunting-park, sent out cards inviting some persons of the best society to a hunting-party. Invitations also came from the neighbors, and Eric was able to be present with Roland at a great hunting-party as often as once a week.

Roland was proud of his father's skill in the chase; he was regarded by all as the leader, and the whole company listened with pleasure to his accounts of grand hunts in America. He had even made a short excursion to Algiers, and there shot a lion, whose skin was now under his writing-table;

it was meant for a sleigh-robe, but here in the country, a merry sleigh-ride was a rare thing.

The supper after the chase, in a large apartment fitted up for the purpose, was always of the merriest sort. The Major was here in his element, and officiated as lord of the castle; he spoke of the evenings which Eric enlivened at Villa Eden by reading the ancient and modern dramas; he never knew before that there were so many fine things in the world, and that one individual man could make everything so plain merely by his voice.

Eric had read aloud almost without exception one evening every week. The impression made upon the hearers was various. The Major always sat with his hands devoutly folded; Frau Ceres reclined in her easy-chair, occasionally opening her eyes, to show that she was not asleep; Fräulein Perini was employed with some hand-work, which she prosecuted steadily, exhibiting no emotion; the Mother and the Aunt sat there quietly; Sonnenkamp had a standing request that they would excuse his rudeness. Turning to Roland, he said good-humoredly,—

"Don't get this bad habit—don't get in the way of having a stick in your hand to whittle."

And so he sat and whittled away, occasionally looking up with a fixed stare, holding the knife in his right hand and the piece of wood in his left; then he would resume his whittling.

Roland always seated himself opposite the reader, so that Eric must look him in the face. Often, until it was very late, Roland would talk with Eric about the wonderful things he had been listening to.

Eric had been reading Macbeth, and he was glad to hear Roland say,—

"This Lady Macbeth could easily be transformed into a witch, like one of those who came in at the beginning."

Another time, when Eric had been reading Hamlet, he was not a little surprised at hearing Roland say to him in the evening, before going to bed,—

"Strange! Hamlet, in that soliloquy, speaks of no one returning from the other world, when, only a short time before, the spirit of his father had appeared, and he appears again afterwards."

One evening, after Eric had read Goethe's Iphigenia, Roland said,—

"I can't make out at all why Manna said once that she was Iphigenia. If she were Iphigenia, I should be Orestes. I, Orestes? I? Why was it? Do you understand Manna's meaning?"

Eric said no.

One evening when the Physician and the Priest were present, Sonnenkamp requested Eric to read aloud Shakespeare's Othello. Eric looked at Roland. Will not Roland be stirred up to fresh questioning concerning the negroes? He had no reason he could assign for declining, and he could contrive no excuse for sending Roland away.

Eric commenced reading. The fulness and flexibility of his voice gave the requisite expression to each character, and he preserved the proper distinction between reading and theatrical presentation. He brought out no strong colors; it was an artistic embodiment that allowed the outlines of form to appear, but gave no coloring; it was not an imitation of life, but a simple outline drawing of the general features, softened but sufficiently defined.

The Doctor nodded to the Mother, as much as to say that Eric's interpretation was very pleasant.

For the first time, Frau Ceres listened with eager attention, without leaning back once during the whole evening; she continued bent forward, and her countenance wore an unusual expression.

Eric read on continuously, and when he was giving the close of Othello's sorrowful confession of guilt, in a voice struggling with tears, like one resisting the inclination to weep, great tears ran down over the pale face of Frau Ceres.

The piece was ended.

Frau Ceres rose quickly, and requested the Mother to accompany her to her chamber.

Fräulein Perini and the rest of the ladies went away at the same time. The men were standing up, and only Roland remained sitting, as if spell-bound to the chair.

Glancing towards the Doctor, the Major said,—

"Isn't this a really wonderful man?"

The Doctor nodded.

The Priest had his hands folded together; Sonnenkamp surveyed his whittlings, placing them in a little pile together, just as if they had been gold-shavings, and even bending down to pick up some that had fallen upon the floor. Now he straightened himself up and asked Eric,—

"What do you think of Desdemona's guilt?"

"Guilt and innocence," replied Eric, "are not positive natural conceptions; they are the result of the social and moral laws of humanity. Nature deals only with the free play of forces, and Shakespeare's plays exhibit to us only this free play of natural impulses in men and women."

"That's true," interrupted the priest. "In this work there's nothing said about religion, for religion would necessarily soften, ameliorate, and rule over the savage natures, conducting themselves just like natural forces, or rather would bring them into subjection to the higher revealed laws."

"Fine, very fine," said Sonnenkamp, who was quite pale; "but permit me to ask the Captain to give me an answer to my question."

"I can answer your first question," Eric rejoined, "only in the words of our greatest writer on æsthetics: The poet would characterize a lion, and, in order to do it, he must represent him as tearing in pieces a lamb. The guilt of the lamb does not come into question at all. The lion must act in accordance with his nature. But I think that the deep tragedy of this drama lies hidden."

"And what do you think it is?"

"This maiden, Desdemona, without mother, brother, or sister, grown up from childhood among men, might love a hero, whose lyric, childlike nature, craving love and clinging fast to her, would make him crouch like a tamed lion at her feet. This submissive strength, renouncing no element of its wild energy, but, as it were, purified and exalted, opens the well-spring of that love which covers everything else with oblivion, overcomes the difference of race, and washes clean out the black color of the skin.

"When Othello kissed her for the first time, she closed her eyes, and he kissed her on the eyes; and her eyes are closed not for one instant merely, but for a long period. But an unparallelled horror, a wild insanity, would be the result of this shutting of the eyes when Desdemona should hold in her arms a child, who should appear, in its whole exterior, strange, abhorrent to her, like some creature that did not belong to the human race. Out from her heart, crushed and trampled under foot, there must have come a shriek of agony. A child upon her breast, a creature so unlike herself! That look, which Hegel describes as the highest of all that the eye can express, the first look of the mother upon the child, that first mother's look must have killed Desdemona, or made her raving mad."

Sonnenkamp, who had all the time been rapidly shifting the whittlings about with his fingers, now threw them all upon the floor in a heap, and went up to Eric, holding both hands stretched out at length. His huge frame trembled with emotion, as he cried out:—

"You are a free man, a freethinker; you are not to be humbugged. You are the first one that ever gave me a reasonable explanation of this antipathy. Yes, it's so. The instinct of the poet is wonderfully prophetic. 'Against all rules of nature!' This is the expression of Desdemona's father, and this is the whole solution of the problem. On this expression the whole turns, and every part is in harmony with it. The result must be, as it is, a product of nature. It's against nature!"

The men who were present had never before heard Sonnenkamp speak in this way, and Roland, who had been staring fixedly before him, looked up as if he must convince himself that it was really his father who was speaking. In an exultant tone, for he observed the effect produced upon them all, he continued:—

"Marriage—marriage! The Romans understood what was meant by that. Where marriage is in violation of nature's laws, there can be no talk of rights of humanity, equality of rights. Apes, with all their boasted reason, nothing but apes, are these silly preachers of humanity, who build up their theories and universal crotchets, without looking at the facts, and know really nothing of these brutes endowed with speech, who are not human beings, but everlastingly apish and malicious! Ho, ho! thou noble friend of humanity!" he exclaimed, striding up and down the room, "Marry thy daughter to a nigger, do that! do that! Be in terror, every moment, that he will tear her limb from joint. Hug a black grandchild! do that, noble friend of humanity! then come to me and harangue about the equality of the black and the white race!"

Sonnenkamp had clenched his fists, as if he were clutching an antagonist by the throat; his eyes flashed, his lips opened, and his jaws snapped together like a tiger leaping upon his prey. He now suddenly placed his hand upon his breast, as if making a powerful effort to hold himself in control.

"You, Herr Captain, and the poet, have taken me somewhat by surprise," he said, with a constrained smile; and then he again repeated that Eric had gone to the root of the matter. That a white girl could not become the wife of a nigger was no prejudice, but a law of nature.

"I thank you," he said in conclusion, turning once more towards Eric; "you have given me a great deal to think about."

The men looked at each other in astonishment, and the Doctor added, in a timid way very foreign from his usual manner, that he must give his assent to this on physiological grounds, for it was a well-known fact that mixed races, in the third generation, became sterile. A separation of the races, however, does not exclude human rights, any more than it excluded human duties; and religion laid them upon all alike.

While saying this he turned towards the Priest, who felt himself called upon to state that the negroes were susceptible of religious conviction, and capable of receiving religious instruction, and that this secured to them the full rights of men.

"Indeed!" exclaimed Sonnenkamp. "Is that the fact? Why then did not the Church ordain the removal of slavery?"

"Because the Church," replied the Priest quietly, "has nothing to do with ordaining anything of the kind. The Church directs itself to the human soul, and prepares it for the heavenly kingdom. In what social condition the body of man, the outside covering of this soul, may be, we have nothing to do with ordaining or determining. Neither slavery nor freedom is a hindrance to the divine life. Our Lord and Master called the souls of the Jews to enter into the kingdom of heaven whilst they were Roman citizens, and under subjection. He called all nations through his apostles, and did not stop to ask about their political condition and constitution. Our kingdom is the kingdom of souls, which are one and the same, whether they live in a republic or under a tyranny, whether their bodies are white or black. We are glad to have the body free, but it is not our work to make it so."

"Theodore Parker takes a different view," Roland suddenly exclaimed.

As if a bullet bad whistled close to his ears, Sonnenkamp cried,—

"What? Where did you find out about that man? Who told you about him? How's this?"

Roland trembled all over, for his father seized him by his shoulders and shook him.

"Father!" he cried out in a manly voice, "I have a free soul too! I am your son, but my soul is free!"

All were amazed. Nothing more would be said about his voice changing.

Sonnenkamp let go his hold, his breast heaving up and down as he panted violently for breath. Suddenly he exclaimed,—

"I am very glad, my son; that's noble, that's grand. You are real young America It's right! fine! splendid!"

They were struck with fresh amazement. This sudden change of mood in Sonnenkamp took all present by surprise. But he went on in a mild tone,—

"I am glad that you were not to be frightened. You have good pluck—it's all right. Now tell me where you found out about Parker?"

Roland gave a true account of matters, except that he said nothing about Parker's name having been mentioned by the Professorin when they were making their calls in the town.

"Why didn't you speak of it to me?" asked his father.

"I can keep a secret," replied Roland. "You've tested me yourself on that score."

"That's true, my son; you have justified my confidence."

"We ought to have gone home a long time ago," said the Major, and this was the signal for the company to break up.

The Major had never felt his heart beat so violently, never when stationed on some exposed outpost, never even in battle, as during the reading; and yet it beat worse, after the conversation had taken so threatening a turn.

He kept shaking his big head, and stretching out with his hands in the air deprecatingly and beseechingly, as if he would say,—

"For heaven's sake, drop this talk! It's not good, 'twill only do harm!"

Then he took another look at Sonnenkamp, shrugging up his shoulders. "What *does* the man mean," he thought, "by talking to us in this style! We wouldn't put a hair in his path; what's the use of stirring us up in this matter! Oh, Fräulein Milch had the right of it, when she urged him to stay at home to-day.

"How comfortable it would be to be sitting in the arm-chair, in which Laadi is now lying! And one might have been asleep two hours ago, and now it will be midnight before one gets home! And there's Fräulein Milch sitting up, and sitting up, till he comes in. It was like being saved, when he took out his watch, and could say how late it was."

The Professorin came back at this moment, and told Roland that his mother wished to see him. Roland went to her.

Eric accompanied his mother and the rest, as they set out for home through the snowy night.

# CHAPTER IX
# THE BIRD OF NIGHT IS SHOT

Eric walked in silence with the ladies. The Mother spoke first, saying,—

"I am glad that here, again, I have words of your father's to support me. Nothing is more weakening and more to be avoided than repentance," he often said; "the acknowledgment that we have made a mistake must come, quick and sharp, but then we must reconcile ourselves to circumstances. I have deeply repented no matter how much good I may do, that I have bound myself to this family so firmly that any drawing back or loosening of the ties is extremely difficult. But now that it is done, we must endeavor to make everything turn out for the best."

The Aunt, who spoke but little, added how painful it was that people over whose lives hung some dark crime were banished, as it were, from the kingdom of the spirit; and must meet everywhere with terrible reminders.

They went on again for a while in silence. High above, from the mountain crest, they heard the screech-owl, the harbinger of extreme cold, uttering his dreadful cry; which rose and died away with a mingled tone of lamentation and of triumph. The party stood still.

"Ah," said Eric, "what trouble Herr Sonnenkamp has taken to destroy all the owls in the neighborhood; but he cannot do it."

They walked on once more without speaking. Everything seems a sign and a portent to an excited mood. Hardly breathing the words aloud, the mother said that Frau Ceres' emotion was incomprehensible. She had thrown herself on her neck, sobbing and weeping.

"I do not know how to explain it," she continued; "there is some deep mystery here, and it troubles me."

Eric told them of what had passed among the men, and how Roland, to his alarm, had spoken of Parker. It was plain that Sonnenkamp wished to erect into a moral system the existing relations of slavery.

"Nothing more natural," answered the Mother. "Whoever stands in such relations all his life long, must make something for himself which he calls moral principle. I cannot help thinking of your father again; he has shown me a thousand times how people cannot bear to confess to themselves that their life and actions are bad; they feel obliged to prop them up with good principles. Yet, as I said, we must be quiet, we have one good young spirit to be led to noble ends; that is our part. Whence it sprang, or through what past life it may have come to us, is not for us to determine. The past is our fate, the present, our duty. There's another saying of your father's; and now good-night."

With a more composed mind, Eric returned to the villa. The owl had flown from the mountain, and was now perched on the top of a tree in the park, boldly sending forth its cry into the air. Eric heard it, and Sonnenkamp heard it in the ante-room of his wife's chamber. There must he, the father and husband, wait till his son came out, admittance having been refused him while his wife spoke to Roland. At last the boy came out, and his father asked him what his mother had said: he had never done so before, but now he felt obliged to do it.

Roland answered that she had really said almost nothing; she had only kissed him, and cried, and then asked him to hold her hand till she went to sleep, and now she was sleeping quietly.

"Give me Parker's book," said Sonnenkamp.

"I haven't got it now; the Professorin took it away from me, and blamed me very much for having read it secretly, and before I was old enough."

"Give my regards to Herr Eric; you have a better teacher than I thought," said the father.

Roland went to Eric's room, but he had not yet returned.

The owl's cry was heard again from the tree-top in the park. Roland put out the light, opened the window, took his rifle from the wall, fired, and the owl fell from the tree. Roland ran down stairs, met Eric, and told him that he had hit the bird; he then hurried into the park and brought the creature in.

The whole house was in alarm. Frau Ceres was awakened, and her first cry was:

"Has he killed himself?"

Sonnenkamp and Roland had to go to her room again, to show that they were alive. Roland took the dead owl with him, but his mother would not look at it, and only complained of having been deprived of her sleep.

The father and the son withdrew, and Sonnenkamp praised Roland for having brought down the bird so promptly and boldly.

Eric went back to his mother, who must also have been awakened by the shot, and he found her still awake; she too had feared that it had been some suicidal shot.

The whole house was in a commotion, and it was some time before it could be restored to quiet.

In his pride at having shot the owl, Roland forgot everything else, and went contentedly to bed and to sleep.

But above in the castle, and below in Sonnenkamp's work-room, lights burned late. Eric sat gazing at the flame, and strange forms moved confusedly through his mind. There was Shakespeare's play, there were all the people who had listened to it; but more than all he tried to enter into Roland's mind; and it seemed a fortunate thing to him, that the boy's love of sport had driven away all wondering speculation from his mind. Action, action alone makes free. Where is it, the great all-liberating power? It does not show itself. Independent of our will, and of reflection, there is a great power in the Past and in the view of God working in it, which alone can bring forth the deed. The deed is not ours, but to be armed and ready is in our power.

At last Eric found rest.

Sonnenkamp paced up and down his great room like a prisoner. The lion's skin with the stuffed head lay upon the floor, and the eyes stared at him, till he covered the head with a part of the skin. He asked himself again and again what he ought to do. This Herr Eric was teaching his son to oppose him, and the Mother, who was always regaling them with sayings of her husband, preserved in spirit, forever calling up, as Pranken says, her husband's wandering ghost, the departed Professor Hamlet—no, she was a noble woman.

But why had he taken upon his shoulders this beggarly family, so puffed up with their own ideas? He could not shake them off, without attracting attention. No, he would make use of them, and then throw them away.

At last, a happy resolution quieted him. We must have new surroundings, new diversions; and then, straight to the goal! The day after to-morrow will be New Year's day. On New Year's day we will go to the capital. With this thought Sonnenkamp also found rest at last.

# CHAPTER X
# PLAYING COURT

The first thing in the morning, Roland wanted to carry the owl, which lay frozen outside his window, to Claus, who knew how to stuff birds.

All the events of the past day seemed to have vanished from his mind, leaving no trace, in the joy he felt in his splendid shot.

"Stop!" cried Roland suddenly, as he was stretching out the owl's wings, "stop; I've just thought of what a man said to me in my dreams; he looked like Benjamin Franklin, but he was thinner. I dreamed that I was going to battle; the music was making a great noise, discordant, and broken by shouts, and every now and then the man said: 'A good name—a good name'—and then there suddenly appeared thousands of black heads, nothing but black heads, a perfect sea of them; and they all gnashed their teeth, and I woke up in dreadful agony."

Eric could not answer, and Roland went on:—

"To-day is the last day of the year; we ought to enter upon a wholly new world tomorrow; I don't know why, but I long to have it so."

Eric laid his hand on the boy's brow, which was feverishly hot.

Roland was summoned to his mother, who wanted him; Eric watched him thoughtfully as he went; he felt also that a new page was to be turned, without knowing what it was to be. He looked towards the door, for he expected that Sonnenkamp would send for him. The man had shown on the previous day such new and strange moods that an explanation was necessary. What would it be? This could not be guessed. As if in a vision, Eric saw Sonnenkamp in his own room, in a state of the greatest excitement, sometimes bursting out violently, then calming himself again. He heard the steps of two people approach his room. Roland entered, holding his father's hand.

"Mother is asleep again," he said, "but there is some news. Eric, we are going to the capital together, to stay all winter."

"Yes, I have decided upon it," said Sonnenkamp, in confirmation, after saying good-morning to Eric, "and I hope that your mother will go with us."

With calm deliberation, he went on to say that gay society would be good for all of them, after the loneliness of their retired life in the country; and, with a watchful look at Eric, he added:—

"We shall meet your friend Clodwig, and his charming wife, at the capital."

Eric looked at him calmly, and said that he should feel it to be his duty to meet all of Herr Sonnenkamp's social acquaintances.

"I have thought much about last evening," began Sonnenkamp, seating himself near Eric. "You are a learned and also a bold man."

His manner was extremely polite, almost affectionate, for he was inwardly happy when he could play the hypocrite; whenever he could make fools of all around him, he felt an elevating and sustaining satisfaction. He was in such good humor that he said to Eric:—

"I hope to convert you; to make you see that the best way of living in the world is to hold yourself a stranger in it, and not to bother yourself about the immediate regulation of the affairs of state."

"In some respects," answered Eric, "Aristotle agreed with you; he lived generally in Athens, having a sort of certificate of residence without being a regular citizen, and without being responsible either actively or passively in the choice of rulers; for only in this way, as an alien, could he live wholly in his ideas."

"I like that. One is constantly hearing something new and sensible of the old philosophers. Then Aristotle was free also to go wherever he pleased? That's good!"

Sonnenkamp looked amused. These learned gentlemen are very convenient; they know how to find great historical reasons for what we do selfishly or thoughtlessly. He smiled in a friendly way, and his smile did not disappear, though Eric explained that what befitted a philosopher like Aristotle very well would not do for everybody; for if every one were like him, the world could not last; who would undertake municipal and state affairs?

Sonnenkamp still smiled. This German pedagogue is a funny fellow, he thought to himself; the very hour before starting on a journey, he is ready for a learned discussion. Looking extremely well pleased, he said to Eric:—

"I am very much obliged to you; one always learns something of you; you are always up to the mark."

Every word was meant to give a stab, but Eric took it quite seriously, and was grateful for the gratitude of Sonnenkamp, who was inwardly excessively diverted by this man, so childishly unsuspicious with all his learning.

He desired Eric and Roland to make the necessary preparations for the journey, and then left the room, a servant having come to say that his gracious lady was ready to see his master.

He entered Frau Ceres' room. She looked at him languidly as he said he was glad she was better, and that she would be able to undertake the journey to the capital on the following day. In glowing colors he represented the pleasant life in the city, upon which they had a sure hold through the family of the Cabinetsräthin, Count Wolfsgarten and his wife, and also through Herr von Endlich's family.

He added in a very confident tone: "Be strong and charming, lovely Frau Ceres; you will return to these rooms a Baroness."

Frau Ceres sat up, and only mourned that the dresses ordered in Paris had not yet arrived. Sonnenkamp promised to telegraph directly, and promised also that the Professorin should go with them, so that the entrance into society could be made under her auspices.

"You may kiss me," said Frau Ceres.

Sonnenkamp did so, and she said,—

"I think that we shall all be very happy. Ah, if I could only tell you my dream, but you never like to hear about dreams, and it is better that I should not tell it. But there was a bird with great wings, enormously large, and I was sitting on the bird, and was carried through the air; and I was ashamed because I was not dressed, and all the people below were looking up at me, and hooting, and shouting, and laughing, and then the bird turned its head round, and it was the Professorin, and she said: You are so splendidly dressed! and then I had all my ornaments on, and my lace-trimmed satin dress—but I know you don't want to hear my dream."

Sonnenkamp left the room in good spirits. The day was bright, a keen, cold, sparkling winter-day, when the whole landscape, every rock, every tree, stood sharply out against the blue sky; the ice had closed over the Rhine, and a strange quiet, like a repressed breathing, lay over the whole scene.

Sonnenkamp was glad that the bright daylight had driven away all the spectres of the night, and brought fresh life. He immediately gave orders in the stable, that two pairs of horses and a second carriage should be sent to the capital. An hour afterwards, as he was walking with Eric and Roland to the vine-clad cottage, they saw the horses, covered with warm blankets, on the highroad, already on their way to the capital. Roland begged that his pony might be sent also, and permission was given; then he asked which dogs he might take, and when told that only one must go he could not decide which it should be.

The Professorin's large sitting-room looked like a yearly fair; on tables and chairs lay great packages of knit and woven woollen garments for men and women. Fräulein Milch was reading from a large sheet of paper the names of various needy people, and a list of the articles intended for them, while the Mother and the Aunt compared the bundles with the list.

When this was done, Fräulein Milch called in Claus, with his wife and daughter, and the Seven-piper with his whole family. They were directed to deliver the bundles to the people to whom they were addressed, and were very ready to undertake the work.

"It's very well that you don't give any money," said Claus; "but there's something wanting."

"What is it?"

The entrance of Sonnenkamp and Roland prevented his replying.

Sonnenkamp expressed much pleasure with the discreet manner in which his money had been used, and spoke a few friendly words to Fräulein Milch, whom he had not seen since the morning when Roland was missing.

He asked for the Major, and learned with regret that he had not been well during the night, and had not slept till nearly morning, so that he was probably still asleep; he had, happily, a constitution which always recovered its tone by sleep.

The Professorin asked to be excused, as she wished to send off the things before she attended to her early visitors; she now asked Claus what he meant by saying that an important thing was wanting.

"Yes," said the huntsman, "Herr Sonnenkamp is just the man for it."

"For what?"

"I mean that it is all well and good to wrap people up and protect them from the cold; but hilarity and joy are still lacking, and I think something ought to be done about warming up inside, and it wouldn't go amiss to send every one of them a bottle of wine. Every year the people see the vineyards before their eyes, and work in them, and most of them don't ever drink, so much as a single drop of the wine."

"Good!" said Sonnenkamp. "Go to the butler, and tell him to put with every bundle a good bottle of last year's wine."

Sonnenkamp was in a most lavish mood, for he put, besides, in each bundle a gold-piece; but he almost spoiled the whole by saying to Claus,—

"You see how much confidence I have in you. I have no doubt that you will deliver it all faithfully."

All the huntsman's jolly good humor seemed damped, but he restrained his anger, and only pressed his lips tightly together.

Roland helped carry the bundles to a cart which was waiting before the house, Sonnenkamp wanted to prevent him, but the Mother made him a sign to let him do it. With the last package, Fräulein Milch disappeared.

In the emptied room Sonnenkamp told the Professorin of his plan of removing to the capital, and begged her to accompany the family.

Gratefully, but most positively, the Professorin declined; and Sonnenkamp had some trouble in hiding his vexation, when he found that no persuasions could change her decision. He took leave politely, but out of humor, and Roland promised to leave Griffin with her as a guard.

The Professorin felt that the boy wanted to be doing something for her while he was away, and to sacrifice for her something which he cared for.

"Life will go well with you." she said, as she pressed his hand.

Roland felt a thrill through his whole being; he had received one of the holiest of blessings, though it was given in such simple words.

The Professorin had promised to come that evening to the villa, where they were all to watch out the old year.

When she came, she found great black chests in the hall; in Frau Ceres' parlor all the chairs were covered with clothes, and Frau Ceres was as happy as a child, directing everything with an activity never seen in her before. At last they all repaired to the dining-room and sat down to tea.

All felt that a great break had come in their life; while the conversation went on easily and continually no one noticed the time, and all believed that it would be very hard work to keep awake till midnight. The Professorin felt the strain, the haunting ghost, if one may so call it, of the impending separation; they were, in fact, no longer here, no longer together. She said more of this than she really meant to, and told them of her entrance into the great world.

Frau Ceres was very attentive, and kept begging her to go on. Suddenly she rose and asked her husband to leave the room with her. Sonnenkamp soon reappeared, and begged the Professorin to do his dear little wife a favor. She declared herself quite ready; and it seemed she was to play the Princess, Eric the Court-Marshal, Sonnenkamp the Prince, and Aunt Claudine the Mistress of Ceremonies. The Aunt resisted the arrangement, and blushed deeply; but the Professorin persuaded her, and managed to make her take the *rôle* of the Princess.

After a little waiting, the folding-doors were opened. Eric stood at the door with a wand, and led Frau Ceres, who glittered and beamed in diamonds and pearls, to the throne of the Aunt.

The Aunt condescendingly dropped very slightly the fan which she held, and Frau Ceres made a truly courtly reverence.

"Come nearer," said the Aunt. "It is very good in you to take up your abode in our country."

"It was my husband's wish," answered Frau Ceres.

"Your honored husband is very benevolent."

"I thank you," replied Frau Ceres.

"If I were in your place," exclaimed Sonnenkamp, "I would say, Your Highness, it is our duty, and we are highly rewarded for it by its meeting your gracious notice."

"Please write that out for me, I will learn it," said Frau Ceres, turning to her husband. She seemed to have grown younger, and her cheeks glowed.

The Professorin was extremely animated, and after saying: "I am your Mistress of Ceremonies," she led Frau Ceres to a seat.

"No, not so,—you must look after your train a little, and spread it out handsomely. So,—that's light, and then open your fan, you have the right to open it now, but not before. It is best to have it hung to your wrist by a small cord; it falls so easily."

The jesting went on merrily; when twelve o'clock struck, Roland cried:—

"Father, now your health is being drunk by hundreds of people."

Sonnenkamp kissed his son, Frau Ceres kissed the Professorin, then bent her head and waited calmly for a kiss on her brow from her husband. Outside, the bells rang, and guns were fired.

"Welcome to the New Year! to fresh life!" cried Eric, as his pupil gratefully kissed the hand which grasped his own.

In the neighborhood of the villa, there was much noise of guns and shouting; and Sonnenkamp was quite indignant that the good German police should allow such doings; it was nothing but rude vulgarity.

Eric said, on the other hand:—

"We can find in this inharmonious noise, if we consider it psychologically, an expression of joy. Without knowing it himself, the insignificant man who fires off a pistol, takes pleasure in the sense of surprise that he can produce an effect so far off, and that so many people must notice what he does. So this custom, barbarous in itself, is to be explained; it gives force to the human voice, you see, to the vociferous shouting."

Sonnenkamp smiled, and Eric was glad that he had brought, not his pupil alone, but the father also, to a gentler view of humanity.

But Sonnenkamp thought: This walking university, these ready catechetical answers on every subject, begin to grow a little tedious; it is well that we are going into a wider circle.

Then he smiled, and bade Eric and Roland a cheerful good-night.

Warmly wrapped in furs and attended by two servants, the Professorin and the Aunt returned to their own house; and soon all was still, and every one dreaming of the New Year.

# CHAPTER XI
# THE ICE BREAKS UP

In the morning, when Eric and Roland were saying good-by at the green cottage, a message came from Fräulein Milch to offer herself and the Major that day, as visitors to the Professorin.

The Professorin praised to aunt Claudine the tact of the housekeeper, who evidently felt that they would be lonely on that day.

It was snowing steadily, and from her closed window the Mother made a sign of farewell to her son and to Roland, who drove by in the first carriage, and afterwards to Herr Sonnenkamp and Fräulein Perini, who bowed from their carriage: Frau Ceres lay in the corner, closely wrapped up, and did not move.

The Major and Fräulein Milch soon arrived. The Major kept himself under strict military discipline, and allowed no slight indisposition to change his stiff bearing; he was rather hoarse, and could say even less than usual, but he offered the congratulations of the New Year to the ladies with as much cordiality as formality.

"This year," he said, "will complete the fifty years that we have lived together."

He pointed to Fräulein Milch, and his hand said, Not a better creature walks the earth. But his looks said still more, which was not so easily understood.

They had a very cheerful dinner, and Fräulein Milch told them how many pleasant things she had already heard about the valuable presents, in the various houses.

The Major forced himself to master his indisposition, to be fit company for the three ladies; he praised the Professorin for knowing how to make such excellent soup, though she was such a learned lady.

"Yes, yes," he laughed, "I've really had to force Herr Sonnenkamp to have soup at his table. You see, if I had to go a day without soup, I should feel as if I were wearing my boots without stockings; the lower story of the stomach is cold."

They laughed at this comparison, and the Major thus encouraged, continued:—

"Yes, Frau Professorin, you know everything; can you tell me how it is that though this day is just like yesterday, we feel that there's something peculiar about it because it's New Year's Day? I feel as if I'd put on clean clothes for the whole year."

Again there was a general laugh, and the Major chuckled, well pleased; he had done his part, now he could leave the others to themselves.

After dinner, the Professorin insisted that the Major must take his nap; she had had the library warmed on purpose, and the Major was not a little proud that he was to sleep in the arm-chair there.

"Ah," he said, "I can sleep as well as the best Professor; but so many books, so many books! it's frightful to think that a man can read them all! I don't understand how it's possible."

The Major slept the sleep of the righteous; but he would have had no rest if he could have guessed what was passing between the ladies.

Fräulein Milch sat at the window by the Professorin, who listened in astonishment as the simple housekeeper said how strange it was that Eric should have consented to read the harrowing drama of Othello; the Major had been driven almost crazy by it, and, besides, there were so many points in it which could not be touched upon in the family.

"Do you know the play?" asked Frau Dournay.

"Indeed I do," replied Fräulein Milch, her whole face flushing to her very cap-border. Then, to the Professorin's surprise, she went on to remark upon the poet's wonderful stroke of art in placing the young married pair on the island of Cyprus, where strong wine is produced and drunk, not always in moderation; for in that solitude, and under that hot sun, wild, burning passions were fostered, too. The greater the happiness of a fondly loving pair on such an island, the more miserable would they be if any discord rose between them.

The Professorin listened as if a new person were speaking, whom she had never known before; but she said nothing of her thoughts, only asking:—

"Do you think then that the play was unsuitable to have been read there because Herr Sonnenkamp has been a slave-holder?"

"I would rather not say more about it," said Fräulein Milch evasively. "I do not like to talk about the man; it rejoices me,—no, that isn't the right word,—it makes me easier that he scarcely notices me, and seems to think me too insignificant to be looked at. I am not angry with him for it, but rather grateful, because it is not necessary for me to look at him; and friendliness towards him would be hypocrisy."

"But you must not turn me off in that way. Can't you tell me why you thought it unsuitable for being read?"

"I cannot."

Aunt Claudine, thinking she saw that Fräulein Milch had something to tell which was not for her to hear, quietly left the room.

"Now we are quite alone," said the Professorin, "you can tell me every thing. Shall I assure you that I can keep a secret?"

"Oh, I am only sorry that I have gone so far," stammered Fräulein Milch, drawing her cap-strings through her fingers. "It is the first time for fifty years that I have paid a visit, or eaten at a stranger's table; I ought not to have done it; I have not yet gained self-control enough."

Her face quivered, and her brown eyes glowed.

"I thought that you looked on me as a friend," said the Professorin, holding out her hand.

"Yes, so I do," cried Fräulein Milch, seizing the hand with both her own, and pressing it with fervor. "You cannot tell how I thank God for having granted me this before my death; since I devoted myself to him, I have renounced all the world; you are the first—oh, I think you must know all, you need be told nothing."

"I do not know all. What do you know of Herr Sonnenkamp?"

Fräulein Milch hung her head sadly, then put both hands before her face, crying,—

"Why must I tell you?" Then she rose, put her mouth to the Professorin's ear, and whispered something. Frau Dournay threw her head back, and grasped the sewing-machine, which stood before her, with both hands. Not a word was spoken. Outside, all was still, except for the cawing of a flock of crows which were hovering over the Rhine.

"I do not think you would tell me such a thing on a mere rumor," said the Professorin at last. "Go on, and tell me plainly how you learned it."

Fräulein Milch looked round timidly, and answered:—

"I have it from the most trustworthy of men, whose nephew has sent a child here to be educated; he knows the name which Herr Sonnenkamp formerly bore, and all about his past life. But, dear, noble lady, why should not a man be able to take up a different life, a new existence, whatever he may have done?"

"Of that another time," interrupted Frau Dournay; "tell me the name of the man who has told you this."

"So be it then. It was Herr Weidmann."

The Professorin covered her face with her hands. "What are you saying of Herr Weidmann?" asked the Major, entering suddenly. "I can tell you, Frau Professorin, that any one who doesn't know that man, doesn't know one of the best and truest men in the world. He's one of God's masterpieces, and God himself must have satisfaction in him; every day, when He looks down from heaven, he must say: The world isn't yet so bad, for down yonder I have my Weidmann; he is a man—a genuine man. Everything is included in that, there's nothing more to be said."

Both women felt a sense of relief in the entrance of the Major, who now prepared to go home with Fräulein Milch. After they had gone a few steps, the Professorin called Fräulein Milch back, and asked in a whisper,—

"Does the Major know, too?"

"Oh no, he could not bear it. Forgive me for having laid such a burden on you. Believe me that it is not made lighter to me, but heavier."

The guests departed; and soon after, the postman brought a letter from the University-town. Professor Einsiedel, who for twenty years had brought his New Year's greeting to Frau Dournay, did not choose to fail in it to-day; they were cordial and significant words which he wrote, but they seemed to come from a different world. Twice she read the postscript, for there was a greeting for Eric, with the message, that the Professor would soon send him a book on slavery which was announced as just published; and he added the exhortation that Eric should finish his work within the new year.

The Professorin looked thoughtfully at the words. What did it mean? Eric had never spoken to her of any such work. She passed her hand through the air before her brow, as if she would drive away every strange thought. A recollection rose within her. This very morning she had been expressing her sorrow to Aunt Claudine that she could no longer dispense any charity of her own, though it was the duty of every one to give from his own store. What she did seemed nothing; only the gifts seemed of importance. Almost involuntarily, she opened the box in which lay the money that Sonnenkamp had intrusted to her. How could she say in future to those who received it: You must not thank me, but Herr Sonnenkamp.

She collected herself, and went to the library, where she stood gazing out of the window. It seemed as if something were actually gnawing at her heart. In spite of inward reluctance, she had allowed herself to be brought into these relations, and her power of clear and intelligent perception seemed clouded.

Down the river there was a heavy roar, with a sharp cracking sound, as if a new world were opening; the ice had broken up. Great blocks were floating down the stream. They were hurled, against each other, turned over, crushed into fragments, brought together again, and floated on. Every block, large and small, was crowned with a wreath of snow, formed by the icy splinters that were ground to powder and thrown on top by the breaking up; the fragments floated down the river so swiftly that one realized, for the first time, how rapid and strong the current always is.

The sun set in a glowing sky across the Rhine; half aloud, the Professorin said to herself:—

"This first day of the year, which is now declining, has brought me a terrible experience; it must be borne, and turned to some good end."